F L Y I N G   W O U N D E D

Contemporary Poetry Series
University of Central Florida

Florida A&M University, Tallahassee
Florida Atlantic University, Boca Raton
Florida Gulf Coast University, Ft. Myers
Florida International University, Miami
Florida State University, Tallahassee
University of Central Florida, Orlando
University of Florida, Gainesville
University of North Florida, Jacksonville
University of South Florida, Tampa
University of West Florida, Pensacola

FLYING

University Press of Florida

GAINESVILLE · TALLAHASSEE · TAMPA · BOCA RATON
PENSACOLA · ORLANDO · MIAMI · JACKSONVILLE · FT. MYERS

W O U N D E D

Susan McCaslin

To Sandy,

may you prosper in all you do.

Thanks for being a great student & remembering me!

love,
Susan

Copyright 2000 by Susan McCaslin
Printed in the United States of America on acid-free paper
All rights reserved

05 04 03 02 01 00   6 5 4 3 2 1

LIBRARY OF CONGRESS CATALOGING-IN-PUBLICATION DATA
McCaslin, Susan, 1947–
Flying wounded / Susan McCaslin.
p. cm. — (University of Central Florida
contemporary poetry series)
ISBN 0-8130-1796-3 (cloth: alk. paper) —
ISBN 0-8130-1797-1 (pbk.: alk. paper)
1. Women—Poetry. I. Title. II. Contemporary
poetry series (Orlando, Fla.)
PR9199.3.M42368 F58   2000
811'.54--dc21   99-086327

The University Press of Florida is the scholarly publishing agency for the State University System of Florida, comprising Florida A&M University, Florida Atlantic University, Florida Gulf Coast University, Florida International University, Florida State University, University of Central Florida, University of Florida, University of North Florida, University of South Florida, and University of West Florida.

University Press of Florida
15 Northwest 15th Street
Gainesville, FL 32611-2079

for Phyllis

The psychology of creativity is in its essence feminine because the creative work of art leaps forth from unconscious depths, that is, from the domain of the mothers.
C. G. JUNG

Contents

Acknowledgments xi

FLYING WOUNDED

Preface 3
Her Mother's Depression Rag 5
Her Mother Designs It 6
Postwar: The White House 8
Bustle Dresses 9
Men Have a Way of Disappearing After the Kids Come 11
I am Sick and You Visit Me 12
Dad's Girl 13
The Cat Did It 14
On the Rag 15
Next To New 16
Hysteric 17
California Dream'n 18
Letting Herself Go 19
Frogs with Sequined Eyes 20
Piano Lounge Queen in Flapper Dresses 21
My Mother's Body 22
Triolet for the Amphetamine Afflicted 23
Devil's Eyes and Voices 24
Catatonic 25
Schizophrenia 26
The Call 27
University Hospital 28
The Rending 29
Head Rifts 30
"I Am Crucified with Christ Yet I Live" 32
Teen in the Back Seat 33
Getting Religion 34
Mistrusting Women 36
Avoiding Silence 37
Fatigued 38
I Go Psychedelic for You (1969) 39

Walking Out of My Mother's Life (1972) 40
Feeding the Ravens of Unresting Thought 41
Don't Put Me in Order 42
In Denial (1982) 43
Mother Blame 45
Talkaholic 46
Mall Bag Lady 47
Chronic Fear 48
Thin and Unable to Swallow 49
Flying Wounded 50
Motherlode 51
Under a Bushel 52
Resurgam 53
What Her Light is Like 54
Now 55
Postscript 56

ISSUES OF LIGHT

1. Numbness and Tingling 59
2. Menopause Poem 61
3. Self-Diagnosis 62
4. Insert 63
5. Father Dream 64
6. Reading Newspapers 65
7. Mother Dream 66
8. Under Investigation 67
9. Rules for Writing Out the Dark 68
10. Clown of God 69
11. Trickster 70
12. Climacteric 71
13. MRI Brain Scan 72
14. Disembarrassed 74
15. Close Call 75
16. Fragility 76
17. Pitted Against Myself 77
18. Improbably Light 78
19. "Lots of Middle-aged Women Cut Their Hair" 79
20. Mindfulness 80
21. Christmas Poem 81

Acknowledgments

The author gratefully acknowledges the editors of the following Canadian periodicals in which some of the poems in this collection first appeared: *Canadian Woman Studies, Ariel, The Antigonish Review, Museletter, Women's Education des Femmes, Wascana Review, Pottersfield Portfolio, The Prairie Journal, Writer's Block Magazine, Afterthoughts, DeFiance, The Rowan Anthology on Depression, Jones AV, Backwater Review, The Carleton Arts Review, Contemporary Verse 2, Dandelion, Room of One's Own, The New Orphic Review, The New Muse of Contempt, Symposium, Beneath the Surface, Kairos II*, and *Exile.*

FLYING WOUNDED

Preface

These poems are and are not autobiographical. They are a poetic transformation of my experience, based on the life of my mother, a woman born in the southern United States (Alabama) in 1921. My mother raised two children in the suburbs of Indianapolis in the 1950s and Seattle in the 1960s. In 1963, she had a "nervous breakdown." Throughout the years of my upbringing, my mother experienced dramatic mood swings that would, nowadays, lead to her categorization as manic depressive. In the early sixties her doctor prescribed diet pills laced with amphetamines for a weight problem. Later, I came across an article published in the early seventies that named this drug and suggested it was taken off the market for inducing schizophrenia in women all across America.

After taking diet pills for at least a year, my mother began experiencing hallucinations and delusions of a religious nature. When I was sixteen years old, she descended into a catatonic state and was conveyed forcibly to a nearby university hospital. There she was treated with experimental, hallucinogenic drugs that the doctor later admitted pushed her further into a psychotic state. After several months of treatment, she was released and advised to remain on medication for the rest of her life. She refused to do so and never saw a doctor again, rejecting even dental work in her later years. My mother described her time at the hospital as similar to that of "a victim of a Nazi concentration camp."

She never recovered from the trauma and remains what society would probably call a "neurotic woman with a severe anxiety neurosis and a multiphobic personality." These poems are my attempt to explore how my mother's experience affected me and to honor her. This is not her story but mine.

The sixties were times of experimentation in the field of psychiatry. Though my mother did not undergo shock therapy, my grandmother and my mother's first cousin received a series of electromagnetic shock treatments, much against their wishes. There are no instances of men in my family who received such treatments. In all cases, the women felt in retrospect that they had been coerced into "therapy" that damaged them irreparably. My grandmother exhibited no sign of mental illness prior to her treatments other than moderate depression at the death of her husband. My mother's cousin was treated for signs of stress related to being a single parent in a time when most women remained in dysfunctional marriages at all costs.

I am not a psychologist and have minimal background in modern psychology. These poems are written out of a desire for greater understanding. They are dedicated to all the many children of such women.

Her Mother's Depression Rag

"Gotta look good—gotta fit in.
If you don't keep yo' looks, girl,
the world gonna do you in;
cream that face; powder that nose,
but most of all keep your figure—
and pull up yo'r hose.

I was a schoolteacher, a lady down south,
then married a man who's out on the road.
I'm sick of scrounging, down in the mouth,
but if he makes it big down in Tennessee
you can have those piano lessons.
And remember, it's just as easy

to love a rich man as a poor man—
easy as lemon meringue pie.
And honey, maybe other girls can
wear that loud red and lemon
but it doesn't suit your type—
wear black: it's slimm'n.'"

Her Mother Designs It

perched like a spider in silk
practicing parlor graciousness
on carefully inspected male boarders.

Along comes the tallest man she'd ever seen
and she just knows he's a good boy
soon as he moves in 'cause he keeps
a portrait of his Mom and Dad on his dresser.
"Any fellow who respects his parents like that
must have had a fine upbringing."

Stepping inside he wants to know
right away, "Are there any girls?"
He has just left the dormitories due to
distractions and wants a quiet place to study.

"Not a one." She bats her eyes;
then keeps my mother sequestered a month,
never explaining when he stumbles
on a pretty, 112-pound girl with silk
stockings and clouds of wavy hair.

"Ask him to the Sadie Hawkins."
So she does and they go, hardly talking.
After, she says she doesn't like him
with his pursed up Presbyterian lips
and she is, anyway, in love with a football player;

then inexplicably seesaws. "Yes, he is
sort of handsome, and nice."

Her mother charms that deadpan fly
three more months till he proposes
after volunteering to go overseas:
"Would you ever consider marrying me?"

"Never turn down a good offer" drums
in her head, "You can always
change your mind later."
"Why yes, I would consider it,"

locks the engagement, snaps the staid ring
on the virgin hand.

Postwar: The White House

It might as well be wrapped in cellophane
it looks so perky with its picket fence,
three-step porch where she poses in her
new black coat and pumps; white, like
the president's house washed over
with post-war optimism.

Here she bakes her first and only
lemon meringue pie which he doesn't
like because his mother always made chocolate
and he prefers chocolate; he catches
the flu and vomits at dinner
into her mother's best gravy bowl,
and her mother swears she will never,
ever eat out of it again, and shakes
her finger right in his face
at which appendage his teeth snap
in a feeble effort to make an unappreciated
joke and regain his dignity.

It is at that table he later explains
we had to drop the bomb on the Japanese
to stop the war and save all those American lives.
"Truman did what he had to do
and a man's got to do what a man's got to do,
especially in war."

She doesn't form an opinion, for wives
are discouraged anyway from talking politics
and there is after all a life romping inside her
to the tune of "keep your sunny side up."

Bustle Dresses

Blustering that he can understand one
but not three bustle dresses,
he flings them on the bed,
fetching in shiny taffeta, cobalt blue,
emerald green, slimming black with polka dots.

"We don't have that kind of money,"
though she says "we aren't hurting."
Spendthrift and tightwad, chained eternally.

She only buys in pairs or multiples
and dresses for herself to some image
of a young, sophisticated cocktail lounge
queen, grad of witty chitchat trying
to recreate college afterglow in a suburban
village of '50s Moms.
No car, hacking coughs, runny noses.

She never gets to those ritzy clubs
except once with her drinking cousin
who drives a Chrysler with tinted glass.
So the bustles bump and grind away
in the closet for ten years
and are finally given to a blowzy neighbor
who can't believe she "had such clothes
cause no one ever saw them."

Her body's pull away from her husband's
touch enunciates clearly enough
that in spite of a penchant for sexy
outfits, nights with prince charming
had been a shock and a disappointment
from which she had never recovered.

In adolescence I never hear,
"Love between a man and a woman
can be a beautiful thing."

Occasionally he blazons he isn't getting
enough and wants more
children, the pleasure of their making,
to which urgency after the second
she firmly shuts the door.

*Men Have a Way of Disappearing
After the Kids Come*

Not that they aren't good husbands and fathers,
aren't there for dinner,
weekend tussles, family vacations
and pouring iodine on open cuts

but if they decide suddenly
its time to join a club
or pull the old clarinet out of the closet
and play in a band on Tuesday nights
or do overtime at the office at double-time
because you need the money

what can you say? He works hard
(not that he doesn't play with the kids);

but who rubs mentholatum on blazing chests
and hushes nerve-jangling coughs
so he can get his sleep?

I Am Sick and You Visit Me

in the night with a wrung cloth,
bundle me in afghans against the chill.
When I develop whooping cough
and can't catch my breath,
mother, you hold me.

During measles and mumps when I am
hysterical, the time I have
a kidney infection so bad
the doctor says afterward,
"We nearly lost her,"
yours is the nearer voice
cutting through my body's
gargantuan landmass, my booming
din of magnified sound.

Only you
call me back with fret and fuss
and fresh-peeled apple slices on a tray.

Dad's Girl

Freud would have relished, Mom,
your marking of my kitten curl
in his lap, arms flung
round his neck. And everyone
says how much I take after him
and his side of the family.
I admit to playing house to him
to supplant you, just to be
your opposite—competent,
adored. How can I help
being apposite—slim
to your bloat, tall
to your slump, quiet
to your heady scattering
voice thrown everywhere?

It is understood
I am Dad's girl,
and my brother
his mother's son.

The Cat Did It

Your friend's husband, shell-shocked,
goes on a monthly rampage looking for dust,
inspecting ledges like a general;
so Bette always keeps her house spotless,
but you let dust accumulate like sand
on dressers, end-tables, a pale coating
to flip a rag at once a year.

You are lady Chaos, First Dust,
comfortable in your element,
so I, your child, have to be a tidiness freak.

(Even today, halfway through a poem
without a dust image anywhere, I'm compelled
to stop word-processing and wipe
the electric radiator lurking under
my desk harboring rampant dust bunnies;
cannot put my feet up after a lecture
until I have raced around to pick up
the fallen stuff and wipe down crumbs
on hands and knees like little Orphan Annie.)

At seven, I make my bedroom formal peace
against your flying barrage of words
and discordant falling objects,
laying out my dolls in aesthetic groupings.

At eight, I stand up to you, hands on hips:
"I'm ashamed to bring my friends to this house!"
and receive an unexpected slap. Your nail catches,
leaving a small, crescent-shaped scar
lasting well past adolescence.

Asked about it by friends I say,
"The cat did it."

On the Rag

At the first soft show of red
you hand me a cotton pad and belt
through a crack in the door
(my blood on the rise
yours in retreat)
and offer no condolences
or congratulations.
Our warm and speaking bodies
do not lie—my breakouts,
your flushes, my estrogen waxing,
yours on the wane.
These hormones that send you catapulting
into frenetic activity then slow collapse
on the upstairs twin bed
leave me confused and dizzy,
though I know I am not dying.

Next to New

Second hand rose,
how can I unforget
the Next-to-New Shop
where you gather cartloads
of variegated garments
in your rounded arms,
drape them over me,
young Persephone
to your dark Demeter?

I want matching cashmere
sweater sets like my friends'
and a pleated skirt
with cheerleader socks
but you fix me up
with '40s-style sweetheart
sweaters and long straight skirts
completely the wrong colors.
Never mind, you can dye them
to match in our archaic washer.

Then you jag my bangs two inches
above my brows, thin them relentlessly,
shouting, "Too thick, too thick!"
Our voices shrill behind coat racks
the day I vow I will disown you,
your clothes; cast off
these castoffs forever
and never let you touch
my panoply of hair.

Hysteric

Shut-in by choice, eremite,
you assume too much air and space
and when you rattle and flush,
one glorious physician indicates
he will be glad
to scoop away your troubles
like pails of red sand,
pare those fluctuating
moods down to size.

The notion spreads like common sense
across your numbness
and you almost say, "yes
yes, anything," except your husband
stomps across the floor
of your weakened will shouting,
"No wife of mine's to be
tampered with when nothing's wrong!"

The doctor drops the case,
writing off in his black pad
"another hysterical female."

California Dream'n

Dad is called down to the place
of dreams where the oranges
and walnuts bounce off the trees
to rescue his blue-eyed father.

A stroke has erased half the man's brain
and Dad's mother is wandering the streets
weeping her husband's name.

He flies them home, deposits them
nearby; finally moves them in
violating his wife's redrawn line.

She clips rose heads, tears grass,
mutilates photos of herself
that she says make her look fat

by scribbling crosshatch lines
around waist and hips. She pops
more pills and more, consumes

the mocha and vanilla ice creams
of malls where she wanders
and begins to live.

They have failed each other's tests
but he has passed his own:
to honor his father and mother

that his life be long.

Letting Herself Go

into harpy, medusa
midnight ice cream reveler

Mom balloons out
puffing and huffing

exchanges her smart clothes
and dyed-to-match shoes

for mismatched patchwork robes
cuts her hair in jagged strips,

indulges screaming fits, occasionally
fixes herself in hall mirrors

(still lipsticked and smiling),
then begins to say the unsayable

to whoever wants or does not want
to hear

"It has finally come to this,"
she hears her mother say,

"She has let herself go."

Frogs with Sequined Eyes

Nine stone frogs "ribbit" in the garage
awaiting the sea-foam unbottled paint,
the scarlet and sapphire sequins
she plants on unembellished eyes.

One day she lowers them,
immobile, to the receiving earth
where they sink, settle
near our stumbling threshold.

Neighbors do not ask
about the amphibian dark
or the artisan hands
that horned and spotted them.

Still they leap, leap
under the princely moon
rewriting their transformations
on the breath of her pacing.

Piano Lounge Queen in Flapper Dresses

All she ever wanted to do, she says,
was tinkle keys at a cocktail lounge,
someplace classy with low lights
where she could small talk the customers
(keeping her distance, of course),
charm them with her razzmatazz

so she brushes up her "Rhapsody
in Blue," her "Jealousy" and "Who's
Sorry Now," sporting a gold lamé
flapper dress with white fringe
and sequins, raising her arms
glittering with enormous laughter.

She dazzles. I half believe because
there is energy in those bones
the house will fall before her.

My Mother's Body

bloated, flabby, with cellulite
in full career, immersed in a sea of foam;

that commodious flesh, something
rejected, dragging behind, forlorn.

"I am not my body," she insists.
"Exercise is hazardous to your health.

Don't exert yourself. Don't strain
the flesh or brain. Ease into cream

pie and grits. All that talk about
protein and a balanced diet—

why I read about a man who lived
to be a hundred and ate pretty much

anything he pleased; smoked too.
The sweet, soft food goes down nice,

is easy on the stomach. Besides,
you're way too thin; nothing to you.

Have another piece of coconut dream cake,
before you fade away." I am grasping,

fading mother, into the crepe of your arms,
the folds of your white skin draped

over my bed; I am swimming through jelly
to the harbor of your yearning bowels.

Triolet for the Amphetamine Afflicted

"Dear Dr. Hormone feed me for my dinner
those little pills so slippery and so cool;
just jazz me up; I want to be a winner.
Dear Dr. Hormone feed me for my dinner
those little pick-me-ups that make me thinner.
You know I used to think I was a fool
till Dr. Hormone fed me for my dinner
those little pills so slippery and so cool."

Devil's Eyes and Voices

One day she is reading the Bible
and all the pertinent texts
raise themselves in yellow light;
filaments of words grow fat with meaning
and a fleshy wing circumscribes her
like a wind. There is a whirring
and she rolls like Ezekiel on her side
acting God's rejection and love for Israel.

Her teenage daughter enters the room
wearing emerald eye shadow slanting up
at the corners. Green eyes smirk.

It's the devil wearing green,
old fool, and her daughter has been
whisked away on a wing and a prayer.

The voices begin chanting ditties,
issuing commands; the television
becomes vatic; ubiquitous eyes
murmur threats and promises.

She is finally at the center of a world.

Catatonic

After the messaging
insidious TV,
the men in the wires
outside your window,
the refrigerator who
(austerest god)
commanded worship
on the groveling floor
at 2 A.M., the rummaging
cupboards, the flying
locusts with their stinging tails

you dissolve yourself perfectly
into transparency.
Things lose their long malevolence
as you attain stasis,
invisibility

and for one moment
the devils envy you
with your husband and children
crouched at your knees
calling your name.

You have no name
and so the white jackets come
and give you a wrist-tag
carry you away
petrified cadaver
to asylum, elysium.

Schizophrenia

(a kind of mental Diaspora
with no one home to pick up the pieces)

"What a silly woman," the voices
say, but God, God, He, surely He
would not say "What a silly
woman." He would say
nothing or, "beloved daughter"
in whom whether or not
I am well pleased
I suffer

and once her father
up from the South peering
through a porthole of the sealed ward,
was God, and sometimes he is
her father, Father untouchable

but her mother blows in witchy, close,
her mother is She-Devil
talking to the psychiatrists,
choking my Mom with smoky eyes.

"Ac-cen-tu-ate the positive
Don't mess with Mr. In-Between;
He the Devil see-saw mind.
Don't mess with him,"

over and over in her head
and she, locked in this leaning
tower like a bloated nun
in some Inquisitional convent.

The Call

Besieged by voices, you are
in Cathar France

where they dizzy you on
the Catherine wheel,

blazon your face among those
cauterized for love,

throw you like a numb metaphor
to Crazy Logos

blast you like a nova
to absolute zero

where the Mercy Seat unseats you,
and Rigor reigns

with dark-tongued Confusion.
Daughter of voices

Daughter of the Voice. (You say)
the problem is

this disquieting inability
to exit yourself.

University Hospital

Thrown in a close cubical three days
you defecate on the floor
and no one comes to clean up;
only bland robotic leers
pierce through opaque cubes.

Sweet southern rose
how your petals pour sweat
when they say you will never
see your children again
without cooperation
which means peeling
more therapeutic potatoes
and submitting to shots
(the drug of the month)
that send you somersaulting
further out into moonscapes
where we cannot, cannot come.

For three months
you tread that broken ward
where human detritus
shuffles and rocks
under priestly medicos
in their clean offices
on the seventh floor
who sometimes remove
their gloves when consulting.

The Rending

My mother rent her flesh. What did her in?
She didn't want to talk or face the wall.
They shut her in a cell and made her grin.
She couldn't eat; she knew her words were small.
She placed her knife and fork with ritual ease.
A black straw for the bad, a white for good;
Unsmiling, joyless Jesus was a tease
who tripped her up; at last she understood
drumming at heaven's gate long before noon
that he must cast her back to do her duty.
"Go serve your family, you're here too soon."
She wrapped herself in scarves, shed her beauty,
till her lost body, strangely light and fine,
sagged like grey laundry hanging from a line.

Head Rifts

beyond the pale   pale lady

"a great gulf fixed twixt
me and thee"

not a Lazarus tongue drop to unparch

we are us   Laz are us
is us

Laser eye

yet I write wanting a center
from which to scribe your lost body

while you explode quicksilver
my crazy Logos hold

words followed by
words words words
mouthed silently
Gestapo commands

It's one thing
to romanticize this craziness
another to lurch
three months in hell
without a hand basket
(*worse than a Nazi*
concentration camp,
you said)

Just because you are paranoid, mother,
doesn't mean they aren't out to get you.

You heard at the gates of heaven
the angels' rat-a-tat hammers
repairing your brain.

If you could have gone higher
would you have heard them singing?

"I Am Crucified with Christ Yet I Live"
(St. Paul)

yet not I to not be suffered to speak,
teach, preach, not I
at this long last table
covering her head
failing to avoid asylum
and the rigors of the garden

but Christ-Joan d'Arc living in me
drowning Her exquisite face
searing Her Amazonian body;
Her cuneiform cantillates in my palms.

I am Her harp stretched out—
She-harp, Muse's Orphan
God's beloved heresy—
I Am She.

Teen in the Back Seat

Never say anything.
Scrunch back and let her
words rattle over you.

One wrong sound, one look
and honeyed titter whips itself
into hurricane; tornado mind
stops at nothing.

Just when she is most
hilarious, every sentence
punctuated by infectious chuckles,
most playful in her T-shirt

with the Garfield tea-towel
hand sewn on her chest,
and that chest rising
with side-splitting mirth

that is the moment
she dips down
(euphoric roller coaster plummeting)
where you (absolutely)
do not want to go.

Better let her winds
fluster themselves
and curl at last
to stupor.

Getting Religion

It has always been there—
that soul deep old time religion.
The psychiatrist blames her psychosis
on being born in the Bible belt.
For years she modernized, adopted
the skepticism of her college profs;
yet when Kennedy died she compared him
to Lincoln, then to God.

Now she is saying God-light has
permuted the fissures of her brain.
She refuses to appear for therapy,
refuses to converse with
the Freudian who wants to blame
everything on her mother;
swishes her medication
decisively down the toilet
because Jesus is her medico,
her head honcho.

She pipes in radio preachers—
Brother Shamrock from down home
still bellowing the Word on tapes
even after his death; hangs out
in charismatic coffee houses
swaying back and forth to "Jesus
Is a Soul Man" and "Rocka My Soul."

We worry about how much money
is being diverted into envelopes
marked "full gospel," how many
times she lays hands on the TV
for healing.

Yet behind all that hype
is something protecting
itself in a star net of something
larger, more loving, something
that makes me want to call her

incipient ecstatic, struggling
outside, not merely cracked.

Mistrusting Women

"Never trust a woman."
She urges her self-betrayal.

"How can you possibly trust
a female gynecologist?

I don't care how much training
she has, she can't cut like a man.

Not that I would let any
of those doctors cut on me.

And I'd never trust a lady
lawyer either; and when it comes

to a good word-spitting preacher,
give me a Bible-pounding man.

It's fine, you being a teacher
and all, as long as you don't

go in for preaching—it just
doesn't look right on a woman."

Avoiding Silence

You enter the world attended
by the gods Ruckus and Commotion
with a radio and TV in every room
going simultaneously all day
and all night, not because
you might watch a program through
but for the steady comfort-thrum
needed to accompany your buzz
and drum; a sound, an image
to focus you, keep you from flying off
into zones where your atrophied artist
watches but never participates
and the ground is rolling
under your unsteady wings
and the angels whisper,

"Let something of her
consciousness remain
till God becomes her ears
and her eyes."

Fatigued

Cushioned into your son's abandoned lower-bunk,
you hunker down for an all-day sleepathon.
Your light snoring fills the room
with hummingbird wings; you are sailing
away from morbid wakefulness.

Your body molds itself to sinuous cloud
and the cross on your brow unstiffens.
These days there is no incessant word-flow,
for almost always you are prostrate,
flattened, incomprehensible.

I Go Psychedelic For You (1969)

If poets are the antennae of the race
and allied with the compacted mad,
there is this compact, mother:
you shall go divinely insane
and I shall go behind you
wearing boa feathers and snakes

Jane Eyre and Bertha
(the madwoman in the attic)
reconciled; two big-time women
passing over the hill hilariously
into language, leagued
companions of the bipolar
disorder, delusions
and paranoias on poles
parading before.

Poets hear their voices too
and obey them just as religiously.

So I will go psychedelic for you mother
in floral skirts and chains
and wear green skippingly.

And when the interviewer asks,
"Is your mother still living?"
I shall answer, "Yes
I am."

Walking Out of My Mother's Life (1972)

No sooner am I in the door
for a respite from grad school
than I'm planning my exodus.
Too much loss of breath here,
my old room sweaty, deranged.

How can I sleep in my bed
with the muttering, the non-
conversations, the "I love
you," one moment and the
"You're with the devil" the next?

"Help me! Don't touch!" you plead.
You are beyond me, mother,
Humpty Dumpty with a broken brain,
and if I get too close
I'll be the one with the irretrievable pieces.

Feeding the Ravens of Unresting Thought
(after Yeats's "The Two Trees")

You sweep by daily in your big Buick
scraping the curb of Penney's back parking lot
where willows droop over cement
and poplars scatter seed.

The hungry, hooded ones with black cloaks
circle you even before you park
your noisy claptrap machine.
Your blue arms now are flapping, flapping
beneath questioning beaks.

Fending off darting eyes and claws,
you cast your bread relentlessly
high, higher into the light
where it is snatched and devoured.

Then, apocryphal, you
remove yourself
curl deep in your metal nest
and nap under a coating of tinted glass
where the ravens of unresting thought
"shake their ragged wings
alas."

Don't Put Me in Order

Don't come around and clean my house.
I can find things where they are
and I like this cloud of chaos
going before me in my desert.
I like my pillars tacked with
handwritten scriptures, and
I know what people think,
how they look at my clothes.
I like my raucous mouth
and my boundless skirts.
You are not to do my laundry
or check my personal hygiene.
It upsets me. And leave
those empty pizza cartons
in the fridge. I may
find use for them.
I am stubborn as Jehovah
and as likely to rage
if you irritate me.

In Denial (1982)

They say your husband, who has endured
your posthumous, post-hospitalized phase,
is dying of a neurological disease.

But you know your war hero, the betrayer
who always loved his mother and dad
more than you, who loved the kids
and never cared for you (you say)
is not dying. His brain is intact,
calculating means and ends, figuring
out how to die without going bankrupt
while his musculature collapses.

You surpass the logic of his body.
He is not dying because Jesus
will heal him and if he seems to be dying
it is because he needs a massive
faith transfusion. So you visit him
in the intensive care facility
where he is not dying as the nurses
stuff food in his face; and if he
wouldn't complain so much about
their inattention and being left
in the halls, he would not die sooner.

So when he dies he is not dead
and you are in love with Jose
the nineteen-year-old busboy
at the mall who sometimes chats
you up and sometimes ignores you.
How could he? I never liked that
Simon and Garfunkel song, Mom,
about Mrs. Robinson because
it patronizes the middle-aged woman,

but here you are in your sixties
in love with Jose,
his tight pants and loose grin,
while my father is dying.

When he who is not dead, is dead
you say after the funeral,
"It's like I never knew him."

Mother Blame

I fall into blaming.
Why, you never even came
to my grads, all three of them,
because academics is a waste
of time and a Ph.D.
won't get you to heaven
and because these things
are "of the world (worldly)"
and make my brother look bad
who always had to follow
behind me in school.

Then come the excuses
about missing my wedding—
the phobias about travel,
even short trips; though
you visit later for events
of less importance.

The one time you surprise me
is when my daughter is born.
Suddenly the doorway
spills you out laughing
and we are for a moment
St. Anne, Mary and child
encased in each other's laps
till you say, "She looks
just like her Dad.
Girls always
take after their fathers."

Talkaholic

I think of setting up an uh-huh machine to take your calls just a tape that responds appropriately to your non-stop monologues at appropriate moments perhaps you would never know the difference God knows how many magazines I've read dishes done and light scholarly works perused while you nattered on and how mean and insensitive I felt later for after all the least we can give each other is our attention but Mom there is never a break in the reportage hardly a break how do you breathe anyway and no real desire on your part for another person in the verbal arena so I learned early to tune you out since the age of seven I read and read myself alone into a world where there could be dialogue became the quiet one for where was there a place for heard speech I tune you out now with these poems just when you say our chats have come to mean so much so put me down as a spiraling yawning ear to be talked at still sympathetic frustrated at the stuff running on the delicate drum these two coffee machines humming into the night one transmitting one receiving and not receiving

Mall Bag Lady

You are a thread away from being
one of the homeless.
Except for your limited resources
(financial and familial)
you would be wandering the streets
or living under a bridge.

Instead you are elder mall rat,
snack bar regular; the young
people know you and how you like
your coffee, how many hours a day
you warm their booth.
You complain they look at you
weird, act friendly, then
give you the brush.

For years, when asked about you
I would say, "Well, she's a bit
eccentric," or "slightly unbalanced,"
never dreaming to tell you
no one wants 80 cents
in exchange for an all-day sit in.

Chronic Fear

You call long distance for the third time today.
My picture fell off the wall, the one with
the sword-of-the-Lord cocktail stick tucked
in the corner. The Lord told you to put it there
as a sign of his double-edged protection;
and the fact of its falling is ominous.

Number one and only son cannot be reached
and you are lonely, lonely in your widowed house.
You cannot call a neighbor or visit a friend
for none of them are to be trusted, and any
attempt I make to arrange outside assistance
will be interpreted as a sign that the devil
has taken up permanent residence in my brain.

You are shaking; you almost passed out;
you shouldn't be alone; but if anyone
comes for a visit you drive them out screaming.

Thin and Unable to Swallow

you seem to be shrinking
in the big car he left you
with its crimson velour interior
and good sound system.

Your head barely crests
the top of the head rest
and you are still licensed
at 73; so you glide at 15 mph
in a 40-mile zone
ignoring the obscenities
of men buzzing past in fast cars.

At intersections you wait
till the traffic has cleared
for a mile in either direction
before venturing out.

Your body, that always
enveloped magnitude,
is now frail, and osteoporosis
slopes your shoulders.

It is strange to see you
thin, just as your mother
would have liked.
In your dreams she still
whispers, "Too bad hon,
you could have been a beauty
queen or a movie star."

You used to enjoy double dip cones
but now you cannot swallow in public.

Flying Wounded

The wounded mother flies out of sepia dreams
with the wound seeping just under her breast.
Umbilical twists in its shroud,
falls at the feet of the wounding grandmother
who will not fix her teeth
whose breath stinks
who no longer cares about her appearance
lets appearances go
gave over caring at forty
in her scarves and flowing robes.

The wounded queen mother laughs but cannot love
yet loves in her way, once telling
the wounded daughter, "You are
remarkable, a remarkable woman."

The wounded daughter in her mad flight
from the wounded mother
holds her heart before her like a crucifix
and none of them understands how the wound began
or where its gaping ends.

Motherlode

What would I bequeath myself
from your hoard (ornate rings,
twisted, multicolored scarves)
my wonderful, crazy mother alive?

How enter again the nest of your belly,
listen for your dire, flimflam song.
If I could look adult into your eyes
asking how you tricked yourself

into this disguise, would I shake
and shake you new, or stand blankly
stammering with hammering fists
at the unbequeathing culture's door?

Under a Bushel

where you have hidden
your tongue of flame
one thin straw catches
and the whole bush ignites,
vermilion crown
trembles going up
speaking *I am am am.*

You crown yourself over yourself
Queen of Losses
which tally less than a feather—
weight of admission
to paradise burning.

Ladybug, ladybug
is it your home
or your children who burn?

Will we rise from your ashes
or fall back into dust,
unkissed light,
treasure buried in a field?

Resurgam

The inscription on Jane Eyre's
mother's tomb read:
"Resurgam."

You are the endless mystery
out of which I rise.
You gave me birth
but I cannot give you birth.

Even on these pages I mark
only a fragment of transformation,
not you, not even your story.

Yet once in a dream a voice
spoke with your voice:
Because you too have a daughter
it is given you to break the pattern.

And all the living and dead ancestors
and descendants held and released
one breath.

What Her Light Is Like

Pearls glimpsed through rain,
yellowed riverfall
hurtling over cliffs
dropping unnamed,
Christ's breastplate's reflection,
drift of wild hair

a strand within
once touched
allowing her to age
backwards to where
the wrong began

Now

through the mirror of distance
you age into me
the turn of your head
and fidget of your hand
my penchant for sweets

for the unattainable

Postscript

I remember your gesture
thrusting away open tins of spoiled food
your stories of the South, and jokes

soft-current speech
memory of inaccurate memory
antithetical to someone else's.

I cannot ask you for the facts
for what are facts to you
who would be annoyed by this

pestering of the past
this uneasy ahistoric chronicle
tale told to hold what lineage

what line against chaos, for love
and the listening stars

ISSUES OF LIGHT

And the word was precious in those days; there was no open vision.
(1 SAM.3.1)

Write, write or die.
H.D.

I

Numbness and Tingling

Christmas happens as it will
and your hands circumscribe
a thousand ribbons and packages.

There is no heroine,
no wise guests nor holy child
when the numbness starts
creeping from arm to arm.
Tingling darts of migratory
anaesthetized birds fly under skin.

Feet are sacks of grain.
Face, a whirl of clay
stuck by quick pins.

Heart hounds and hams it up.
Breath moves hard.
Mice are playing on your spine.

You tell yourself it is a virus,
back, or nerves, who knows what.
Hormones, female trouble,
time for the small white
doily on the head
like Aunt Susie wore
in '56 when she went weird.

You vibrate like a pipe organ.
Sensation alternates with non-sense.
You are sensationally troubled.
Rat tat, the hammers race
over knees and arms jumping
politicly on command.

With your symptoms it could be
neurological, of course.
But the specialist is off for Christmas,
puts your soft dilemma on hold.

You are as skittish as a pregnant virgin.

2
Menopause Poem

A pause in the menses,
catching breath.

For what?

3
Self-Diagnosis

Though you were educated for something else,
why not play doctor for awhile?
After all, your catalogue of ailments
makes fascinating reading
and you can regale your friends for hours
with a veritable potpourri of symptoms.

Start with the head-wrenching migraines,
the night sweats when you drift
in a sea of your own bodily fluids,
the palpitations and blurring of vision.

You used to read real literature
but now you find yourself gravitating
to the health section of new age bookstores.
That fuzzy feeling and the innocuous music
once disdained, has a certain soft appeal.

You are not clinically depressed,
but troubled by spasms of weeping.
This is not a breakdown
for you haven't missed a single day of work.

Low estrogen levels and quiet attacks
of unaccountable blushing at Dept. meetings
indicate you are undoubtedly pre-menopausal.
But this is more than the onset of menopause.

Perhaps you are not dying.
Perhaps you will only be permanently incapacitated.
Perhaps you are just what the medical books used to call
a hysterical female.

4
Insert

You try to stuff yourself into a box.
Your body is stuttering long slow syllables:
"Dying alive dying alive dying alive
Attend, attend!"

You peek inside the dream window
at feet rising and falling in a sea of glass
from a great distance
and turn away.

5
Father Dream

Each fear an ephemeron;
each day interminable
while it lasts.

No matter how they quip,
"Worry won't help,"
you reel out horrors
as if imagining the worst
somehow wards it off.

And certainly you curse
your boggled imagination
that opens in dreams
of your father's corpse
crawling toward your bed,
feverish and thin with Lou Gehrig's

begging to enter your womb
and be reborn into the world.
But you will not, will not
heft that legacy
however his pale eye begs.

However unknowingly
he planted his curse
by repeating: "I hope
you don't inherit this disease,"
all you ever registered was:
"Inherit this disease,
inherit this disease."

6
Reading Newspapers

You hawkeye the page
for the latest disease report:
"Epidemic reaches epidemic proportions!—
antibiotic-resistant bacteria rampages
China heading to North America!—
AIDS spreads through dental equipment!—
Cure found for cancer
but not available till 2020."

You could be dead by then—
well dead—and with two women
on the block masectomized
it is just a matter of time.
Sooner or later the body
will rebel against itself.

Your invulnerable twenties persona
died with your father.
Anything that has happened to anyone
can happen to you
and is more than likely to do so.

"Don't waste your time worrying,"
you lecture you. "Carpe diem."
Why me? Why not me? Why anyone?

"There's nothing wrong with you,"
your six-year-old remarks casually.
The crease takes up permanent residence
in your brow
as you reexamine your breasts.

7
Mother Dream

Already in your freighted dreams
you cannot lift yourself,
your hands are iced lead,
muscles atrophied, body skeletal.
You roll and crawl past yourself

while your daughter hears you crying in the night.

Already in your febrile dreams
you are sixteen and your mother
(broken, speechless, exactly your age now)
is being carried away to the mental ward

while you hear yourself crying in the night.

8
Under Investigation

The word "hypochondriac"
briefly crosses your mind,
but you dismiss it
with a flick of your
pill box.

The neurologist takes your
bilateral numbness and tingling
in all four extremities
and up and down your spine
quite seriously.

It even wakes you at night
and makes it impossible to do buttons.
You are dead and alive
with sensations to prove it.

He hovers at your knees and joints,
tap, tap, tapping with his
close silver hammer.
Reflexes jump reluctantly.
"Can you walk this line,
push back my arms?
cross your fingers
in front of your nose
without losing your balance?"

You bait yourself in the wait room
preparing for the dark word
but are summoned to the news
you seem perfectly fine.

He orders more tests.

9
Rules for Writing Out the Dark

When there is no opening,
no orifice except what you would imagine
if you could imagine sun,
yourself whole, siphoning honey,

absolutely, do not
summon spectres,
scare yourself to death.

When angel wings desert stone
and your heart is a flat vibrating stone,
idle dumb tongue,

refuse (absolutely) to replay
the tabloids' desolations.

Instead, breathe light.

Let it in, well in.
Catch sparks on the tip of your pen
and throw them high
past the closed intent of your quarters.

Make windows where no windows were.

10
Clown of God

Eyelids fall. Drapery rises
on a stage where Jesus
(actually sandaled and in white)
tells me to lay out my fears.

The words, "incapacitated like my father"
bolt from my lips, transform
into a gigantic metallic block
settling on the planks at Jesus' feet.

Fear two—"Getting older without
accomplishing the task"—plummets,
followed by three, four, five, six,
and the seventh, gargantuan—
"FEAR ITSELF."

Seven cubes align in dark
and I am straining, pushing them
an inch or so towards him,
but I cannot heft their weight.

"Excellent," he signs,
sailing the first over his shoulder
as if it were a balloon.

then lifts the others offstage one by one,
twirling the last and lightest
on his fingers.

A second later out pops his head from the curtain:
"Don't worry, I have blown them all to dust."

11
Trickster

You have had the sight
but erased it from your hours.

You have heard the word
but stuffed it in the ground.

Hermes the Trickster
has again stolen your cattle.

Mary, after the angels,
disbelieves the stone.

Prometheus on the rock
sees Heracles but still groans.

You have had the vision
but do not wear it in your bones.

Climacteric

> Among them was a woman who had suffered
> from hemorrhages for twelve years.
> (MARK 5.25)

(Gk.climakter, rung of a ladder)

She with her geranium blood
hidden beneath her gown,

a nameless woman, diseased?
Perhaps only suffering

a difficult and prolonged
climacteric. She dared to touch.

She with her issue of blood.
He with his issue of light.

Clearly the issue between them was love
and by that ladder she climbed.

13
MRI Brain Scan

After the spinal tap and the electrodes
the giant brain scanner seems quite benign
sleeping in its own interiority.
You dress in the shapeless green
costume that leaves you genderless,
a half of something
whole, wheeled into dimness.

You are an oven-bound loaf of bread.
Don't think for a moment of torture.
Technology is all for your benefit.
They are launching you into inner space,
your body a provisionless craft.
They will take you there and bring you back.
All you have to do is try not to blink
or swallow, and breathe very regularly.
Soon they will chart the firing
of your neurons and electrons.

Giant magnets pulse
from bow to stern
though you feel nothing,
lying in ceremonial stillness
broken only by the periodic bombardment
of bullet sounds ratting and tatting.

Between assaults, the nurse speaks
through a microphone—"How are you
doing?" and you whisper brightly into yours,
"Not too badly."

Some people get claustrophobic.
One woman was too fat to slide inside
this narrow tunnel of dark light.

You are very very calm.

It doesn't bother you that the doctors
conceal themselves like the Wizard of Oz.
But why does no one come into this room?

You are released (solitary, untouched)
into dazzling spring sun.

Two weeks later the doctor phones.
"Don't bother to come in—
I've never seen a more normal brain."

14
Disembarrassed

unburdened, undeceived
you are actually ok.
or if not quite well
then not what you thought.

What will you tell your colleagues,
supportive and tolerant friends?
How will you reimburse your husband
for talking your phobias down,
holding you in the irremediable dark.

You will have to emerge,
assume the usual responsibilities,
court your sense of humor.

There was nothing wrong
except what might pay a sneak revisit—
the usual psychosomatic imbalance
that makes you if not normal
then as ordinary as
humble pie.

There was much wrong
and you are mistaken to deny
your body's faithful articulation.

15
Close Call

You are an escapee
from slow dismemberment.

What you imagined just
failed to fall.

If you had awakened
to the nightmare's teeth

would you have ridden
that horse down

the only road
into the only present?

16
Fragility

Smile mask in place
you carry yourself
on stilts
tall as a Wedgwood chamber

dancing the porcelain woman
erect
who is cool
and pale as white silk.

17
Pitted Against Myself

Scanning the fissure of clay and clay.
Who made the rift but I?

A spirit, fearless, undivided
coming to claim me
makes pomades and spices
from the conflagration of lilies
at the end of the debate,
a spirit, fearless, undivided
whose curriculum is joy.

When She reads the summation,
epitaphs unwrite themselves
flowering on stone.

18
Improbably Light

in uncertainty, the middle of,
the living one shows herself crosswise
Joy

the cross's only crux—
rood into goldenrod.

A woman with her
head in her knees
parsed by light.

Her angel flexes.
Love and fear divorce.

19
"Lots of Middle-aged Women Cut Their Hair"

says Germaine Greer, and she should know
though hers is longish on the back
of her book *The Change*.

So what is the opposite
of a Samson complex?
Not Delila sans scissors,
but one who gratuitously and on a whim
shears her own luxuriant, weighty head
after wearing it long
more than twenty years.

Run your hand over your crop.
Laugh when your daughter calls you spike head.
Luxuriate in the wind
as your face rises from its mass.

20
Mindfulness

You cannot know what's coming.
Why arm for disaster?

Disarm, disgrace yourself
if necessary
but be in your place
as the globed magnolia.

You are not the first or the last
to change.

Christmas Poem

Out of the deer-stepping wild
one of the moss-tipped tribe stole
wings, swallowed light, flew higher
than any had flown from that wood,
unbarren, singing, married the land
and became bridal sheath, wholly apparent,
appareled, white as a wand,
found the babe, unwrapped and parsed her
to the world all without dividing
a single hair.

Susan McCaslin is a poet and an instructor of English and Creative Writing at Douglas College in Coquitlam, British Columbia. She is the author of five books of poetry—*Locutions* (Ekstasis Editions, 1995), *Light Housekeeping* (Ekstasis Editions, 1997), *Veil/ Unveil* (The St. Thomas Poetry Series, 1997), *Letters to William Blake* (M[O]ther Tongue Press, 1997), and *Oracular Heart* (The Hawthorne Poetry Series, 1999)—and the editor of the anthology *A Matter of Spirit: Recovery of the Sacred in Contemporary Canadian Poetry* (Ekstasis Editions, 1998).

CONTEMPORARY POETRY SERIES
UNIVERSITY OF CENTRAL FLORIDA

Mary Adams, *Epistles from the Planet Photosynthesis*
Diane Averill, *Branches Doubled Over with Fruit*
Tony Barnstone, *Impure*
Jennifer Bates, *The First Night Out of Eden*
George Bogin, *In a Surf of Strangers*
Van K. Brock, *The Hard Essential Landscape*
Jean Burden, *Taking Light from Each Other*
Lynn Butler, *Planting the Voice*
Cathleen Calbert, *Lessons in Space*
Daryl Ngee Chinn, *Soft Parts of the Back*
Robert Cooperman, *In the Household of Percy Bysshe Shelley*
Rebecca McClanahan Devet, *Mother Tongue*
Rebecca McClanahan Devet, *Mrs. Houdini*
Gerald Duff, *Calling Collect*
Malcolm Glass, *Bone Love*
Barbara L. Greenberg, *The Never-Not Sonnets*
Susan Hartman, *Dumb Show*
Lola Haskins, *Forty-four Ambitions for the Piano*
Lola Haskins, *Planting the Children*
William Hathaway, *Churlsgrace*
William Hathaway, *Looking into the Heart of Light*
Michael Hettich, *A Small Boat*
Ted Hirschfield, *Middle Mississippians: Encounters with the Prehistoric Amerindians*
Roald Hoffmann, *Gaps and Verges*
Roald Hoffmann, *The Metamict State*
Greg Johnson, *Aid and Comfort*
Markham Johnson, *Collecting the Light*
Hannah Kahn, *Time, Wait*
Susan McCaslin, *Flying Wounded*
Michael McFee, *Plain Air*
Richard Michelson, *Tap Dancing for the Relatives*
Judith Minty, *Dancing the Fault*
David Posner, *The Sandpipers*
Nicholas Rinaldi, *We Have Lost Our Fathers*
CarolAnn Russell, *The Red Envelope*
Penelope Schott, *Penelope: The Story of the Half-Scalped Woman*
Robert Siegel, *In a Pig's Eye*
Edmund Skellings, *Face Value*
Edmund Skellings, *Heart Attacks*

Floyd Skloot, *Music Appreciation*
Ron Smith, *Running Again in Hollywood Cemetery*
Susan Snively, *The Undertow*
Katherine Soniat, *Cracking Eggs*
Don Stap, *Letter at the End of Winter*
Rawdon Tomlinson, *Deep Red*
Irene Willis, *They Tell Me You Danced*
Robley Wilson, *Everything Paid For*
John Woods, *Black Marigolds*